In the Beginning

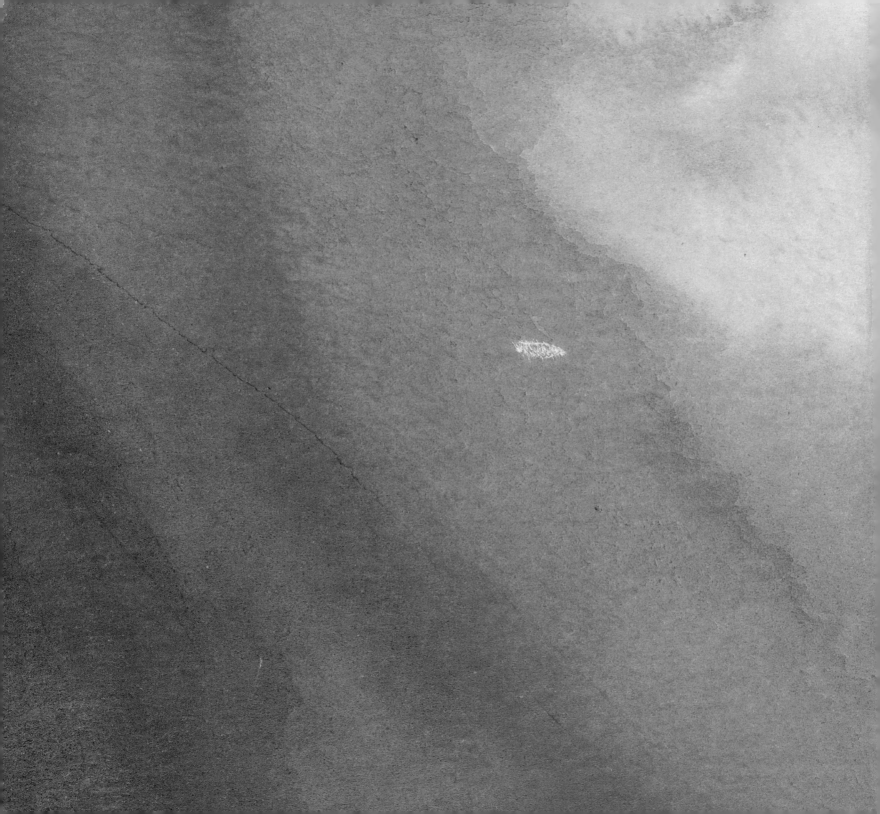

To Tomi-Joe Turner, Charlie Turner, and Jasper Cashmore

First Augsburg Books edition. Originally published as *In the Beginning* copyright © 1997 Lion Publishing plc., Sandy Lane West, Oxford, England.

ISBN 0-8066-4363-3
AF 9-4363
First edition 2002

02   03   04   05   06   1   2   3   4   5   6   7   8   9   10

In the Beginning

Retelling by Steve Turner

Illustrations by Jill Newton

God said WORLD

and the world spun round.

God said LIGHT

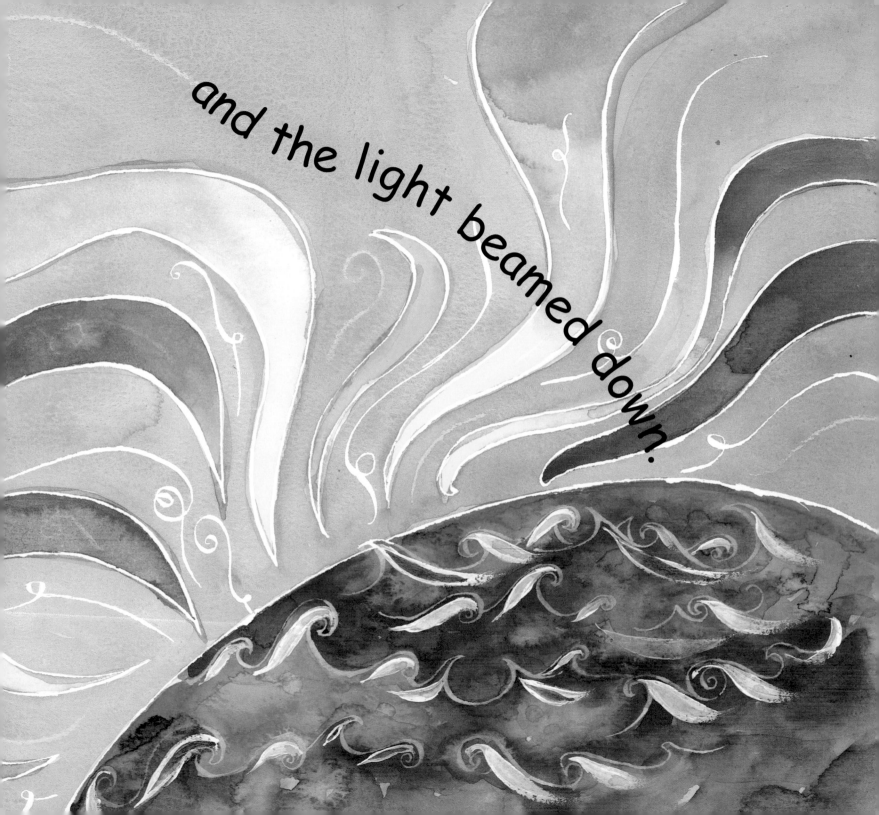

and the light beamed down.

God said NIGHT
and the sky went BLACK.

God said LAND

and the sea rolled back.

God said LEAF

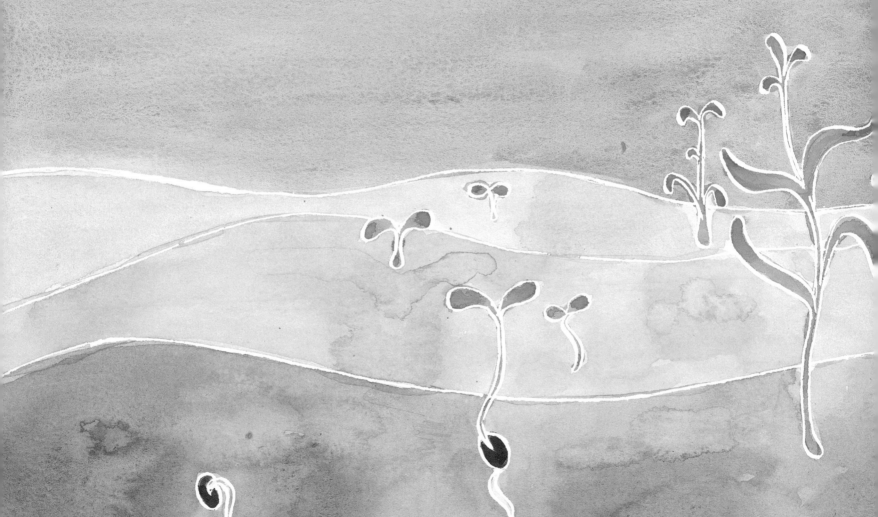

and the shoot pushed through.

God said FIN

and the first fish **grew**.

God said BEAK
and the bright birds
soared.

God said FUR

and the jungle ROARED.

God said SKIN

and the man breathed air.

God said RIB
and the girl stood
there.

God said GOOD and the world was great.

God said REST

and they all slept late.